T0198783

My First ABC Book:
Integrated with Multiple Intelligence Activities

Kan Tsai Tan

ISBN
978-1-5437-4870-3 (sc)
978-1-5437-4871-0 (e)

Print information available on the last page.

To order additional copies of this book, contact
Toll Free 800 101 2657 (Singapore)
Toll Free 1 800 81 7340 (Malaysia)
www.partridgepublishing.com/singapore
orders.singapore@partridgepublishing.com

01/09/2019

PARTRIDGE

My First ABC Book:
Integrated with Multiple Intelligence Activities

Say the picture. Then read.

Aa

A, a, a for Apple

Bb

B, b, b for Butterfly

Trace with your finger and say.

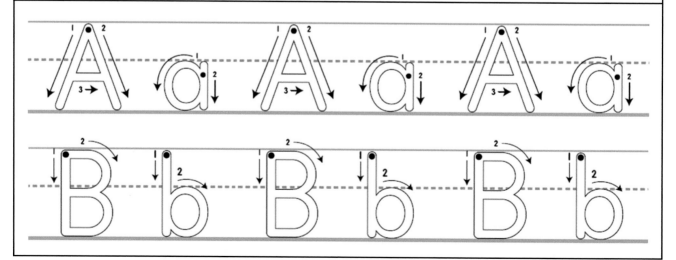

I'm trapped.
Help me to find the way out.

Tips: Tracing will help developing psychomotor skills in little children.

Say the picture. Then read.

Cc
C, c, c for Cat

Dd
D, d, d for Dog

Trace with your finger and say.

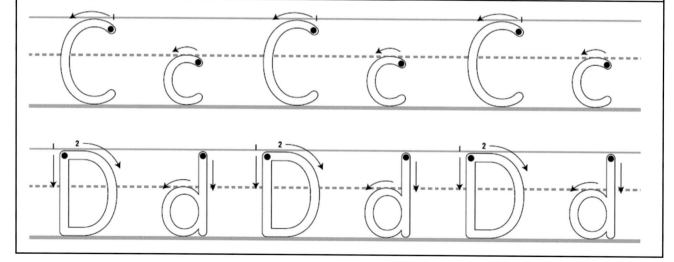

Who am I?
Which is my shadow?

Tips: Increase children general knowledge and vocabulary by introducing these animals.

Say the picture. Then read.

E, e, e for Elephant

F, f, f for Fish

Trace with your finger and say.

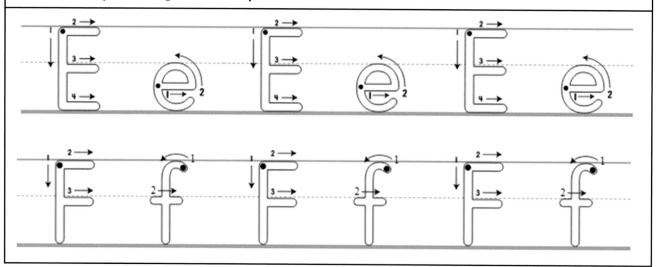

Complete the patterns.

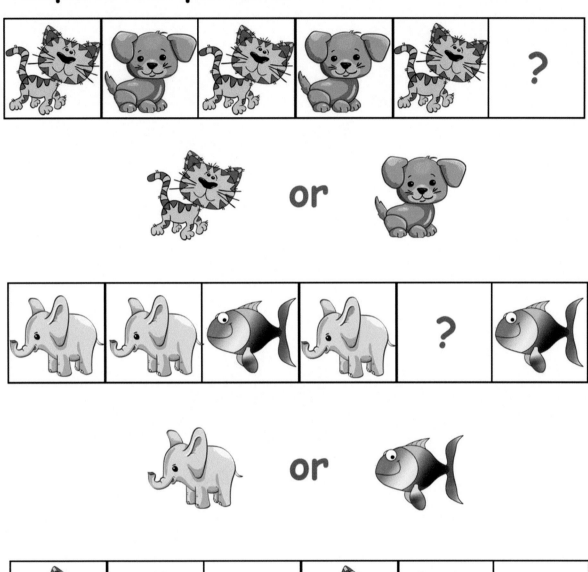

 or

Say the picture. Then read.

Gg

G, g, g for Grapes

Hh

H, h, h for Honeydew

Trace with your finger and say.

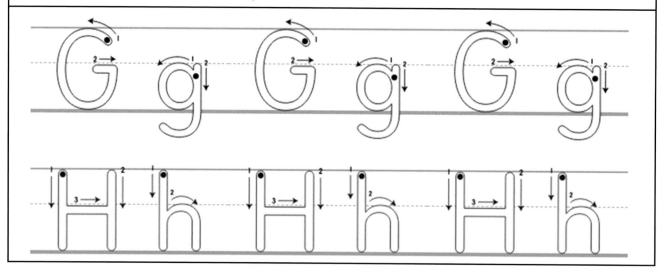

Match the fruit with its juice.

Tips: Introduce these fruits to little children to increase their vocabulary. Introduce colour at the same time.

Say the picture. Then read.

Ii

I, i, i for Ice-cream

Jj

J, j, j for Juice

Trace with your finger and say.

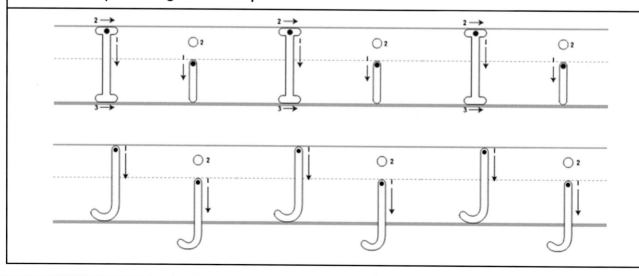

Find 3 unhealthy food.

Tips: Introduce food and help them to understand healthy and unhealthy food.

Say the picture. Then read.

Kk

K, k, k for Key

Ll

L, l, l for Lion

Trace with your finger and say.

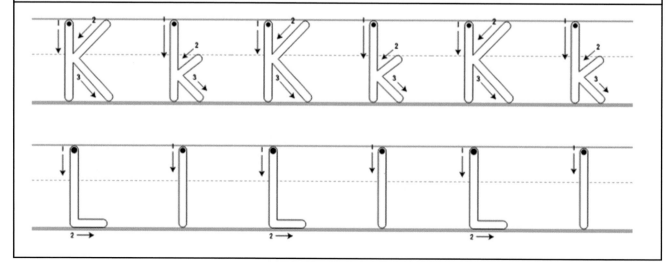

Match the keys to the locks.

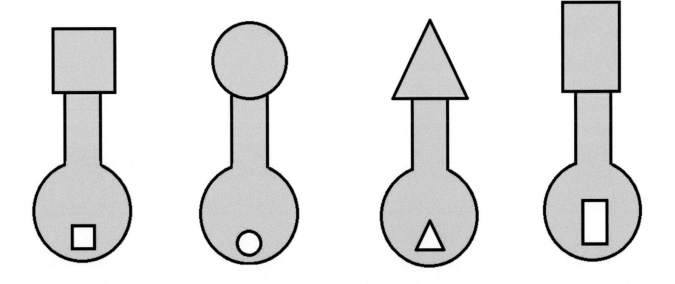

Tips: Introduce basic shapes to children. It would be fun to relate some shapes around them.

Say the picture. Then read.

Mm

M, m, m for Monkey

Nn

N, n, n for Nail

Trace with your finger and say.

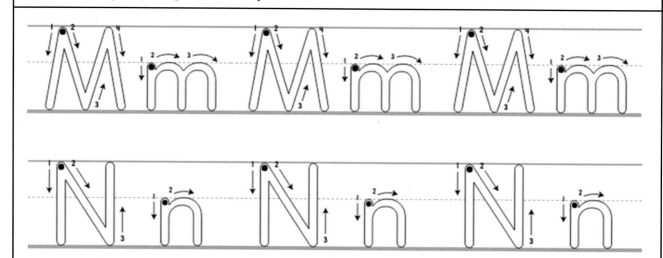

How many monkeys and bananas in the picture?

Tips: If your child have not introduced to numbers, count with him/her.

Say the picture. Then read.

Oo

O, o, o for Octopus

Pp

P, p, p for Penguin

Trace with your finger and say.

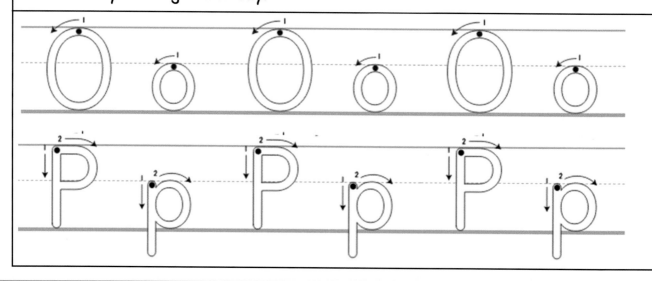

Spot 10 differences

Tips: Guide children to spot the differences and give justification to their answer by asking "why".

Say the picture. Then read.

Qq
Q, q, q for Queen

Rr
R, r, r for Rabbit

Trace with your finger and say.

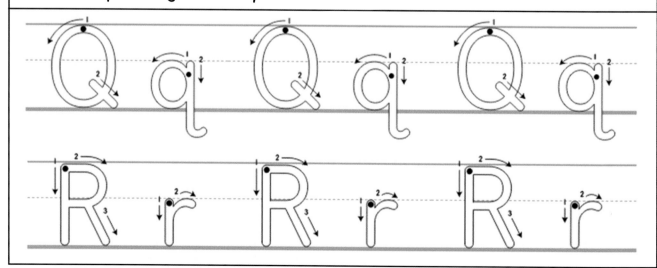

Tips: Little children may need to use their imaginative skills to find the missing pieces.

Say the picture. Then read.

Ss

S, s, s for Ship

Tt

T, t, t for Train

Trace with your finger and say.

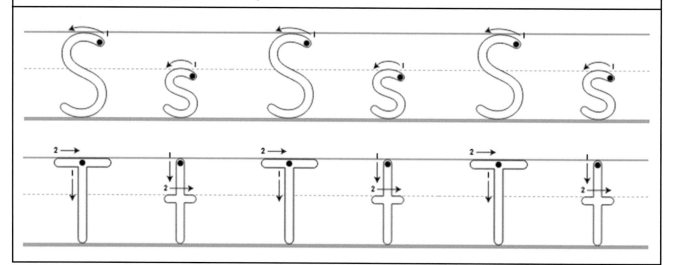

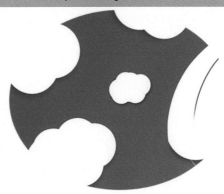

Match the vehicles

Tips: Introduce means of transport. Example: sea, road, railroad, air.

Say the picture. Then read.

Uu

U, u, u for Umbrella

Vv

V, v, v for Vase

Trace with your finger and say.

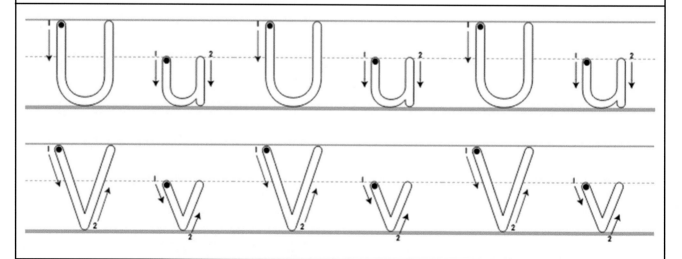

Find the objects below.
1. Umbrella
2. Vase
3. Clock
4. Lion
5. Bicycle

Tips: Guide little children to find the objects by giving cues. Example: On the desk; Near to the lamp.

Say the picture. Then read.

W, w, w for Watch

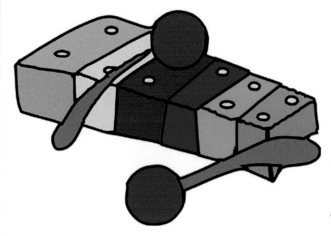

X, x, x for Xylophone

Trace with your finger and say.

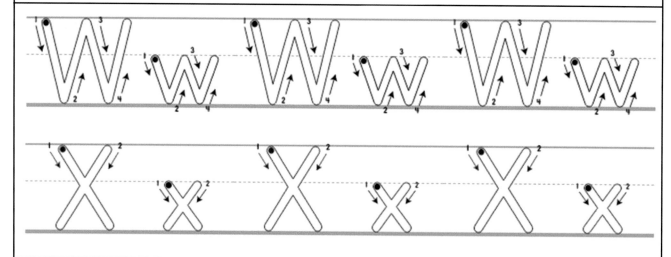

What time is it
Mr. Wolf?

It's _____ O'clock.

□ o'clock

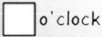

□ o'clock

□ o'clock

□ o'clock

□ o'clock

It's lunch time!
Run!!!

Tips: Add some fun while conducting this activity
by catching the child when he/she say "TWELVE".

Say the picture. Then read.

Yy

Y, y, y for Yacht

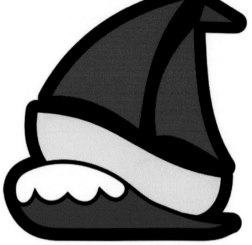

Zz

Z, z, z for Zoo

Trace with your finger and say.

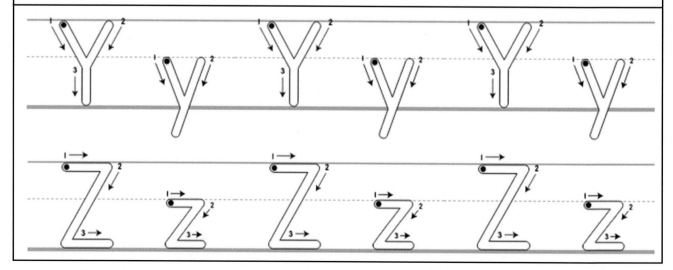

1. Which is the tallest?
2. Which is the biggest?
3. Which is the cutest?
4. Which is the king?

5. Which do you like most? Why?

Tips: Questions 3 to 5 are subjective. Let children answer creatively.

Let's Revise.

Aa

Bb

Cc

Dd

Ee

Ff

Gg

Hh

Ii

Jj

Kk

Ll

Mm

Nn

Let's Revise

Printed in the United States
By Bookmasters